# The Future of Postal Services

**ROBERT ALBON**

*Visiting Fellow, Department of Commerce,*
*University of Birmingham*
and
*Department of Economics,*
*Australian National University*

IEA

Published by
INSTITUTE OF ECONOMIC AFFAIRS
1991
SECOND IMPRESSION 1993

First published in July 1991

Second Impression July 1993

The Institute of Economic Affairs,
2 Lord North Street,
Westminster, London SW1P 3LB

© THE INSTITUTE OF ECONOMIC AFFAIRS 1991

*Research Monograph 47*

*All rights reserved*
ISSN 0073-9103
ISBN 0-255 36247-1

---

All the Institute's publications seek to further its objective of promoting the advancement of learning, by research into economic and political science, by education of the public therein, and by the dissemination of ideas, research and the results of research in these subjects. The views expressed are those of the author, not of the IEA, which has no corporate view.

---

*The Institute gratefully acknowledges financial support for its publications programme and other work from a generous benefaction by the late Alec and Beryl Warren.*

Printed in Great Britain by
Goron Pro-Print Co. Ltd.,
Churchill Industrial Estate, Lancing, W. Sussex
Filmset in 'Berthold' Univers 9 on 12pt Medium

# Contents

| | page |
|---|---|
| FOREWORD *Geoffrey E. Wood* | 5 |
| THE AUTHOR | 8 |

**ONE:**
**Introduction** — 9

**TWO:**
**Postal Reform in Britain** — 12
  Degrees of Competition — 13
  The EC's Green Paper—Delays and Difficulties — 14
  New Zealand's Bold Reforms — 15
  Interconnection — 17
  Towards Privatisation? — 18

**THREE:**
**An Efficiency Analysis of the Effects of Greater Competition** — 20
  1. The Effects of Removing the UK Postal Monopoly — 20
     Letters — 20
     Parcels and Premium Services — 25
     Cost Efficiency — 25
     Dynamic Efficiency — 27
     Combat Predation — 28
  2. The International Context — 28
  Summary: the Benefits of EC-wide Competition — 29

**FOUR:**
**Do Postal Services Constitute a Natural Monopoly?** — 30
  1. Modification of the Model — 30

2. The Degree of Contestability in the Postal Industry    32
      Sunk Costs    32
      Customer Tieing    33
      Access to Technology    34
      Anti-Competitive Strategies    34
      A Market Test?    34
   3. The Empirical Evidence on Overall Economies
      of Scale    34
   4. A Disaggregative Approach to Economies of Scale    36
      Collection    36
      Sorting    36
      Transport    38
      Delivery    38
   5. Economies of Scope in the Postal Industry    39
   6. Is Natural Monopoly an Obstacle to
      Postal Competition?    41
      Economies of Scale    41

**FIVE:**
**Continued Cross-Subsidisation as a Basis for**
**Statutory Monopoly**    42
   1. Letting Prices Adjust    42
   2. Director Subsidies from Explicit Taxes?    43
   3. The Mechanics of Direct Support    44
   4. The Way Forward    45

**SIX:**
**Policy Options in Britain**    47
   1. The Implications of Different Possible Outcomes    47
   2. Is More Competition Inevitable?    50

**SEVEN:**
**Conclusion**    52

TABLE 1: The Letter Process    37

GLOSSARY    54

REFERENCES    57

SUMMARY    *Back cover*

# Foreword

In 1983 the Institute of Economic Affairs published *Liberating the Letter: A Proposal to Privatise the Post Office*, by Ian Senior. In his conclusion to that paper the author wrote:

'The changes which would follow the abolition of the letter monopoly... would be of clear benefit to the urban and the major commercial users of postal services.... Rural users already endure a worse service than urban users—with fewer deliveries, collections and post offices. With the Post Office's monopoly and uniform pricing, the rural user has no means of obtaining a better service even if he is willing to pay more for it.... The Post Office ... does not require the crutch of an archaic and near-obsolete monopoly. It requires the spur of rivalry as a privately-owned company competing with others. The benefits to the British people would be considerable if we were permitted to enjoy competing and privatised postal and counter services.'[1]

Ian Senior reached these conclusions by an analysis of the impact of current and immediately prospective technical change in the mail services. In the present *Research Monograph*, Robert Albon reaches the same main conclusions, but, very strikingly, by a completely different route. His careful analysis of the *existing* structure of costs and markets leads him to the conclusion that competition in postal services is feasible, and that allowing such competition would bring benefits to consumers and, perhaps surprisingly, to the British Post Office.

At the heart of his argument is an examination of whether postal services have to be provided by a monopoly. He carefully examines that claim, and shows by analysis and evidence that it is false.

The phrase 'postal services' covers a wide range of activities. Many of these activities—delivery of leaflets, of local free newspapers, of urgent parcels—are already undertaken by competing suppliers. This gives choice to the consumer and stimulates the supplier to increase efficiency. Dr Albon argues that

---

[1] Ian Senior, *Liberating the Letter*, Research Monograph 38, London: Institute of Economic Affairs, 1983, pp. 47-49.

allowing unrestricted competition over the full range of postal services would bring the same benefits over that full range of services.

The idea that there should be competition in the delivery of letters may seem startling—surely, it will be said, such competition would produce wasteful duplication. In Section 4 that claim is refuted. The provision of postal services is an area of activity which it is easy for firms to enter; there are not high costs which have to be incurred before any business at all can be carried on. And for the same reason, if it turns out not to be profitable, the activity is not costly to give up. There are not large and irrecoverable sunk costs. In summary, the structure of costs in the industry makes it naturally competitive, not naturally monopolistic.

An inevitable consequence of such competition is that it would no longer be possible to subsidise some activities from the monopoly profits earned in other areas. There would be *no* monopoly profits.

At the moment Britain (like almost every other country in the world) has letters delivered at a common charge regardless of how far they have to travel and how isolated the collection or delivery point. Such a price structure does not reflect costs; it is formed and maintained by subsidies. What would happen to rural deliveries if subsidies for them could no longer be obtained from monopoly profits? Robert Albon shows that there are several possibilities. One is that favoured by Rowland Hill. Hill, although the founder of the Penny Post, actually preferred not a uniform charge for delivery, but a charge based on costs, and therefore uniform only when costs were—as he estimated them to be within and between major towns. Outside these urban areas, costs were and charges should be higher. Another possibility is to pay an explicit subsidy from general taxation. This has two important benefits. It avoids the arbitrariness of levying the charge to subsidise rural mail users primarily on urban users of the post. And it makes the subsidy public. Such a subsidised service need not be a monopoly. Rural mail users could thus have the opportunity to pay a higher charge for a faster, or in some other way superior, service whenever they wished to use one, or to pay less for a slower service, perhaps with less frequent collections and deliveries.

The reforms proposed by Dr Albon are not as dramatic or as radical as they may seem at first glance. Britain already has one of the most competitive (and, as he shows, most efficient) postal services in the world. What is proposed is an extension of a process which is already well advanced. Activities which are peripheral to the provision of postal services, or are attached to them by accident of history, have been separated. Post and Telecoms were separated in 1981, and the Girobank separated and privatised in 1989. The minimum charge which can be levied by private courier to deliver an item has not been raised since 1982, and has thus fallen substantially in real terms. This charge could be cut explicitly. It could then be discovered whether a narrower differential above the first-class letter charge generated sufficient demand for there to be competition in that market.

Other possibilities are to allow a competing 'second courier'—a structure akin to the relationship between British Telecom and Mercury—or simply to open up the entire market to whoever wished to enter. Although apparently the most radical, the last is, Dr Albon suggests, perhaps the most appealing. For if a well-established firm faces competition in one part of its business, it is both easy and tempting for it to use profits from elsewhere to cut prices in that area so as to destroy the competitor. If facing competition across a wide range, such a pricing policy would not be possible. Regulation—with its well-known difficulties—would therefore not be necessary.

The benefits to the British economy would not, Dr Albon argues, end with a more efficient domestic postal service. Dr Albon observes that '... the Royal Mail has shown considerable interest in greater competition in Europe'. The 1992 programme should lead to there being free trade in services throughout Europe. The delivery of mail is a service. There should soon be a very substantial market open to an efficient supplier of postal services. The British Post Office is already well placed to take advantage of that; Dr Albon argues, very convincingly, that his proposals would make it even more likely to benefit from this opportunity.

The Institute of Economic Affairs is a Research and Educational Charity. The Institute, its Trustees, Advisers, and Directors must be dissociated from the analysis and conclusions of this *Research Monograph*. But they are very pleased to offer this vividly written and clearly argued contribution to informed discussion and debate.

*July 1991*                                PROFESSOR GEOFFREY E. WOOD
                                                    *Editorial Director*

# The Author

ROBERT ALBON, originally from Melbourne, is a senior lecturer in economics at the Australian National University and a visiting fellow in the Department of Commerce at the University of Birmingham. He joined the ANU in 1976 and completed a doctorate as a staff candidate. Prior to this he worked for a short time at the Industries Assistance Commission in Canberra. His research interests lie in the economic evaluation of public policies encompassing public utility pricing, public sector performance, occupational regulation, housing, taxation, agricultural and financial markets, telecommunications and postal policy.

Dr Albon's work on postal economics has covered many aspects (pricing, competition, performance, history, etc.) in Britain, Australia and Japan. His work on the postal industry in Britain is extensive, including *Privatise the Post* (Centre for Policy Studies, 1987), and Aims of Industry's *Postal Monopoly in Europe: The End in Sight?* (1991). A monograph on Australia's postal industry *(Private Correspondence)* was published by the Centre for Independent Studies in Sydney in 1985. He has a paper on 'Postal Rate-Making' in Crew and Kleindorfer's recently published *Competition and Innovation in Postal Services*, and in 1990 he wrote a report on postal pricing in Japan for the Institute for Posts and Telecommunications Policy in Tokyo. His writings on postal economics have also been published in *Applied Economics, History of Political Economy, Lloyds Bank Annual Review*, and other journals.

## Acknowledgements

I have benefitted from discussions with officials of the DTI, HM Treasury and the Post Office; David Thompson of London Business School; Graham Mather, Martin Summers and Cento Veljanovski of IEA; Pat Hanlon of the University of Birmingham and participants at a seminar in the Department of Commerce, University of Birmingham. I am solely responsible for the contents.

R.A.

ONE

# Introduction

Virtually all countries in the world retain postal services which are government-owned, have a high degree of statutory monopoly, and have a uniform geographical price on *letters**. Britain shares these broad characteristics. However, as has historically been the case, Britain has been one of the leaders in postal reform, emphasising the key areas of competition and organisational change. The 1981 *British Telecommunications Act* was a significant landmark, splitting posts from telecoms and injecting significant competition. Nonetheless, statutory monopoly remains a major obstacle to alternative suppliers and the Post Office remains as one of only three major nationalised industries still under full government ownership. Is there a case for further liberalisation of the UK postal industry?

The advent of 1992 and the completion of the *Single Market** in Europe provides an opportunity for completely opening up *all* European postal services to competition. In one sense it is difficult to see that '1992' does not *oblige* the EC to remove statutory barriers to competition. However, the likelihood is that the major legal monopolies—on 'letters' and printed papers—will remain after 1992. The European Commission seems set to take only a small step towards liberalisation; this conclusion is based on the reports of the contents of its forthcoming *Green Paper*[1] on postal services.

If liberalisation is not going to spring from an EC initiative, Britain itself could act to deregulate its own postal industry. It is argued in this *Research Monograph* that liberalisation is desirable for two broad reasons.

o   Firstly, a freer postal market will result in significant efficiency

---

*Words and phrases set in italics followed by an asterisk, as here, are defined and explained in the Glossary, below, pp. 54-56.

[1] The *Green Paper* was scheduled to go to the Commissioners in June 1991 and then to be released later in the year.

gains relating to pricing, costs and innovativeness. Already Britain's relatively free regulatory structure is matched by a relatively efficient industry, but further advance is possible.

○ Secondly, Britain can help force the EC to pursue its statutory obligation (under the 1987 *Single European Act*) to liberalise and undermine the European Commission's attempts to 'harmonise', possibly including an EC-wide uniform letter rate. The Post Office could clearly benefit from expanded opportunities in Europe and British postal users could clearly lose very substantially from harmonisation.

Even the Post Office itself appears to be changing its stance on liberalisation. Traditionally a strong opponent of demonopolisation and privatisation, elements in the organisation are now making deregulatory 'noises'. This is an odd source of such an initiative which may have been expected from the Minister or his Department, rather than from the Post Office itself. The Royal Mail appears to perceive both the opportunities of a true (i.e. competitive) single market and the dangers for Britain from harmonisation. I will refer at a number of points to the unpublished 'Post Office Plan' for liberalisation and rationalisation of the British market, and the opportunities for Britain to penetrate the European market.

Section 2 reviews the development of postal policy in Britain in the last decade and suggests some possible routes to greater competition, less regulation and more privatisation. I examine what has been happening in other countries in Europe and also in the new 'market leader' in liberalisation, New Zealand. Competition could be expanded by lowering the threshold of private activity (as in New Zealand), licensing a second national operator (as suggested by the Adam Smith Institute (1991) and in the spirit of the first round of telecommunications deregulation), and/or through encouraging *interconnection*\* with the Post Office network (as suggested by the Post Office itself). Limited liberalisation could come in the wake of the EC *Green Paper*. The choice of regulatory framework would depend crucially on which route is followed, but it is difficult to envisage a totally *laissez-faire* system. Privatisation must also be on the agenda, but it does not constitute a major issue in this *Research Monograph*.

Section 3 presents the positive case for competition in postal services, based on the theoretical expectation that competition will result in benefits of static, dynamic and cost efficiency, and on the empirical observation of the effects of introducing peripheral competition in many countries, including the UK. New Zealand, which is scheduled to lift its monopoly almost entirely in 1992, will provide the world's first case of virtually complete demonopolisation. This is an experiment that is being watched very closely in many quarters. Section 3 also considers the international aspects of establishing a truly competitive single postal market in Europe.

One of the traditional objections to competition, *'natural monopoly'\** in the form of *economies of scale and/or scope\**, is discussed in Section 4. This argument has been raised in a host of countries over the decades whenever demonopolisation has been contemplated. There has been a strong debate on this in Britain over many years. Now it has been raised again, by the Commission, in the European context. It is argued here that there is no reasonable objection on economic efficiency grounds to putting natural monopoly to the market test, either in an individual country or in the whole EC. The potential gains are great and quite probable; the potential costs small and unlikely.

Statutory monopoly has also been rationalised on the ground that it allows a system of implicit taxes and subsidies called *'cross-subsidisation'\**. In Section 5 I present an alternative to direct subsidisation, based on explicit taxes, if there is a desire to continue favouring some users while promoting greater competition. This solution has been raised in national debates on the question, and is equally applicable in response to the European Commission's justification of monopoly on this ground. There is a strong danger that following the Commission's course would mean Britain could find herself at the wrong end of an elaborate European-wide tax-subsidy arrangement.

Section 6 concentrates on the options available to Britain, suggesting that its first-best policy has three strands: to liberalise substantially in Britain; to push for overall demonopolisation in Europe, at the very least for intra-EC letter traffic; and to urge the complete rejection of 'harmonisation'.

## TWO

# Postal Reform in Britain

Britain has always been a pioneer in postal reform, including the consolidation of the state's monopoly in the 17th and 18th centuries, and the introduction of a uniform geographical letter rate in 1840. In more recent times the British Government has been unusually active in liberalising the postal industry with a form of corporatisation in 1969; splitting posts and telecoms in 1981; greater competition through the £1 threshold and special licences in 1982; the internal division of the Post Office after 1986; and the privatisation of Girobank in 1989. The extent of this liberalisation can be best gauged by considering the recent changes in Britain concurrently with those occurring in other European countries.

The 12 member-countries of the EC display a marked diversity of regulatory and institutional arrangements in the postal industry, ranging from a significant degree of liberalisation (the UK and the Netherlands) to a more traditional closed market (Italy and Ireland). Germany and France lie between these extremes, largely as a consequence of major reorganisations in the last couple of years. International traffic in *parcels** and *premium mail** are basically free areas, but national attitudes on other items of international mail differ, again ranging from relative freedom to tightness.

All of the member-countries have moved, or are moving, to a form of corporatisation of postal services, primarily involving a split of postal and telecommunications services and placing the postal service on a more businesslike footing. Here again, the UK was the pioneer, principally through the 1981 *British Telecommunications Act*. The Netherlands has also been relatively advanced in its reorganisation. Corporatisation—and independence from telecommunications—effectively means that postal services should become self-supporting except where subsidised directly to perform specified community services. However, the links are not yet broken in all countries. Even one that has split, Germany, retains an interim arrangement to transfer profits from telecommunications to support postal losses. Further, postal services and post banks remain linked in some countries, and there is some evidence that the French and the Dutch post banks' profits are used to keep letter prices down. Corporatisation is far from complete in many EC countries.

None of the postal services has been privatised, at least in core areas. However, reform has sometimes meant hiving-off the postal banking operation and, in two cases, transfer to the private sector. Britain's Girobank has been sold and the Netherlands Postbank has been merged with another bank, effecting a form of privatisation. Furthermore, according to A. J. Scheepbouwer (1990) of Dutch PTT Post, 'It is not unlikely that the state will sell a minority share [of PTT Post BV] to the public in the next few years' (p. 5). In Britain there has been some recent press speculation[1] about the likely inclusion of sale of the parcels and counters divisions of the Post Office in the next Conservative Manifesto. The letters division appears to remain a 'sacred cow', although it has not been explicitly ruled out as a privatisation target.

**Degrees of Competition**

Those countries with the most liberal attitude on structure and ownership are also those with the fewest restrictions on competition. All countries have allowed competition (both internally and internationally) in parcels and some definition of premium mail; although some only recently and, in the cases of Italy and Spain, only under pressure from the European Commission. Most countries regulate on the basis of weight, with threshold levels set at from 500g to 7kg. The UK allows all items charged at a minimum of £1 to be carried privately; the Netherlands has a similar threshold level. Spain allows private carriage of some local business mail (e.g. bank statements) and the Correos' local pricing structure reflects this competition.

Another recent institutional development is the setting up of the International Postal Corporation (IPC) by a number of the major official services. The Corporation, trading as UNIPOST, aims to compete with the international *courier** companies by providing a similar type of service. While this development seems innocuous enough, it could be the first step towards an explicit cartel of

---

[1] For example, articles in the *Financial Times* of 5 and 11 March 1991.

national postal services. As noted by Gröner and Knorr (1990, p. 26), it is

> 'a decisive step in the direction of a single monopolistic "Euro-Post-Office" which would be beyond any public or political control ...'.

Although it is a member of the IPC, the Royal Mail has shown considerable interest in greater competition in Europe. The organisation is apparently 'feeling its way' in the face of significant uncertainty about the regulatory framework in which it will be operating.

**The EC's Green Paper—Delays and Difficulties**

The European Commission has taken a very long time to produce even draft sections of its *Green Paper* on the future of European postal services. The paper was originally scheduled for release in 1989 but has still not appeared. This delay may reflect the political sensitivity of the issues with two strong groups taking opposing positions on the desirable course of policy. On the one hand, there is 'business', both as a consumer of postal services and as an alternative supplier in the market. Broadly, although not without exception, the business interest is in favour of significant demonopolisation. On the other hand, there are the existing postal administrations of most countries, usually allied with recipients of *cross-subsidies**. This grouping tends to favour the continuation of statutory monopoly and its associated structure of cross-subsidies. The Commission has also had to heed the spirit of 1992 which, literally interpreted, requires that free trade in services—including postal ones—should be established. Caught in the middle of these opposing forces, the Commission has attempted to steer a middle course. Unfortunately for the Commission, a 'compromise' can end up by pleasing no-one. The Commission's present position on postal services is emerging as just such a case.

The Commission's approach is a strange mixture of deregulation ('liberalisation') and regulation ('harmonisation'). The province of competition would slightly be expanded, but the realm of regulation would also be widened and would change hands. The role of regulator would no longer lie with national governments and/or postal services themselves, but would pass into European hands. The EC would have responsibility for determining the threshold between monopoly and competition, arbitrating on *predatory pricing** allegations and regulating *terminal dues**. Once in place, changes in demand, technology, and so on would necessitate continuing review of the regulations, then firmly controlled by Brussels. Perhaps even more significant is the decisive trend towards uniformity of price and quality throughout the EC, a trend which has major dangers for the UK, and for the cause of competition.

For a variety of domestic reasons, and in an attempt to avoid the costs of an EC-inspired cementing of statutory monopoly to achieve harmonisation, Britain should liberalise the postal industry if it has efficiency as the primary objective. There are alternative ways in which competition could be introduced, some regulation will be required, and further privatisation seems necessary as part of a package of postal liberalisation.

### New Zealand's Bold Reforms

In New Zealand there has been very rapid policy change on the postal industry. As described by Toime (1991) and Prebble (1989), the process began with corporatisation (removal from departmental control and separation of posts from telecommunications and the post bank), making explicit the subsidisation of rural counter services (Section 5), substantial privatisation of counter services, and gradual reduction of the threshold of private activity to just double the standard letter rate (i.e. 80 cents against 40 cents) by December 1991. As Toime observes, 'the expectation is that full deregulation would occur when the 80c level was reached' (p. 276). There have also been explicit exemptions from the monopoly, including permitting a broadly-based document exchange and the legalisation of the delivery of their own mail by firms.

Britain could follow New Zealand on its approach to competition, as this would continue an existing trend. The £1 threshold, established in 1982, has been eroded in real terms but is still about 4½ times the first-class rate. A document exchange system was also legalised after the 1981 *British Telecommunications Act*. Apart from the reduction in the real threshold there has been no policy change for nearly a decade. The Secretary of State could reduce the threshold to, say, 40 pence and make explicit further exceptions to the monopoly. The New Zealand example of exemption of firms carrying their own mail would, for example, allow British Telecom employees to deliver telephone bills and Lloyds Bank staff to distribute bank statements. Meanwhile, it would be interesting to observe how private mail companies responded to a 40 pence threshold. The existing one is obviously too high to encourage development of a market segment in between the Post Office's first-class service and the various 'premium' and *express\** services. A number of firms (such as London Penny Post) have attempted unsuccessfully to enter at around £1. A larger-scale 'middle-market' service around 40-50 pence may not be viable, but this can be determined only through a market test. Rather significantly, the 'Post Office Plan' reportedly favours a lowering of the threshold as part of a package of suggested reforms.[1]

A second means of introducing more competition could be the licensing of a second national carrier to operate a complete letter service. This has been advocated by the Adam Smith Institute (1991) and seems to have support amongst the aspiring large premium carriers like DHL and TNT. The latter company's Managing Director, for example, has suggested such an approach (*cf.* Jones, 1991). This appears to be the wrong method to employ. Rather than more competition, it could easily result in a two-firm monopoly—a duopoly—somewhat like Australia's recently abandoned 'Two-Airline policy' or Britain's 'Two-Telecom policy' (which is about to be removed). Other potential suppliers would be prevented from offering 'letter' services and there would necessarily be a suppression of potential 'niche' operators.

A third approach would involve a complete opening up of the postal market to competition by means of the Secretary of State issuing a 'general licence' to operate. This is by far the most radical alternative, without precedent in the postal or related industries. Perhaps New Zealand's liberalisation of telecommunications comes closest to a generic example.

In all cases, the Post Office would be given considerable freedom of pricing. However, in the first and the third cases, issues of regulation could be rather important. Firstly, there could be the

---

[1] The Post Office Package apparently involves significant new competition through lowering the threshold and the encouragement of interconnection. At the request of the DTI, the Post Office employed Ernst and Young to advise it on the possibility of separating the first- and second-class services (*Financial Times*, 25 June 1991). Reportedly, the splitting of the services is administratively and financially feasible. The Post Office's response is that it would be prepared to accept much greater competition (e.g. a threshold of 25 pence) on first-class service if it could compete on a level playing-field. The Post Office would require independence on first-class pricing and would be prepared to guarantee maintenance of a national service only on second-class mail.

question of predatory pricing, a major concern of the *Green Paper*. Obviously a powerful 'incumbent', especially one with some 'reserved' areas, could prey on new entrants by unfair pricing. This possibility would be less the greater the realm of competition—the Post Office could not simultaneously wage battles on several fronts, but could easily 'pick-off' a single entrant if unconstrained. Ordinary competition law might be sufficient to prevent predatory behaviour, but there is also the possibility of an Office of Posts (or 'Ofpost') being established to regulate the industry. Like Oftel, Ofpost would have a role relating to interconnection, the second main regulatory issue.

**Interconnection**

Interconnection is concerned with the situation in which one service-provider has access to the network of another service-provider to facilitate part of the overall service. Access of this kind has been a major factor in telecommunications deregulation in various countries. In some cases (e.g. Britain and the United States) the terms and prices of interconnection are regulated by a specific agency. In New Zealand, in contrast, regulation is more arm's-length through recourse of an actual or potential interconnector to the provisions of the *Commerce Act*. This issue is a difficult one and it could arise in at least two important postal contexts. First, if a franchising approach is taken to rural provision, local operators will require access to the Royal Mail network. This is discussed further in Section 5. Second, local delivery may be a problem area for some entrants and interconnection with the Post Office reticulation system may seem desirable. Again, access might have to be subject to direct or indirect regulation, as in the telecommunications case. I return to this second interconnection issue in Section 4.

The Post Office Plan foreshadows a very open approach to interconnection. Indeed, at the premium end of the market and in international *remail**, there is already substantial interconnection. The *Universal Postal Union** (UPU) frowns upon remail activities where acceptance of such items by a postal administration is deemed to have harmed another official service operator. The development of remail has exposed serious weaknesses in the UPU's 'system' of terminal dues. These have been based on the *total* weight of mail carried for another country's postal service, irrespective of the number and weight of individual items. Charges have apparently also been set below *avoidable costs**. The authors of the *Green Paper* are working on cleaning up this messy system and their findings may be useful in helping to establish an approach to other instances of interconnection.

**Towards Privatisation?**

There is, of course, the issue of actual privatisation. A package of postal reform would involve at least some privatisation if the largest possible benefits are to be achieved, because of the market disciplines inherent in private ownership. Competition and an appropriate organisational structure are necessary first steps towards privatisation. There has been limited progress on the first, and considerable progress on the second, of these prerequisites to privatisation. The organisational changes have been discussed in Albon (1987), and this treatment is updated and extended in a paper by Michael Corby.[1] Corby employs an intimate knowledge of the Post Office's structure to make some useful observations on the details of restructuring such a complex organisation.

The organisational structure that currently exists would allow one immediate privatisation, that of Parcelforce. As noted in a later section (Section 4.5, below, pp. 39-40), parcel and premium services have been almost totally separated from the rest of the Post Office and operate in a totally competitive environment. In these circumstances there is absolutely no reason to delay its complete transfer to the private sector, thus adding it to the previous successful Post Office privatisation (Girobank). There is also a very strong case for privatising the Counters Division of the Post Office. Most of its work has already been contracted-out to private operators (the sub-postmasters), and there would be advantages in having the management structure exposed to the discipline, imposed by the possibility of take-over if performance is unsatisfactory, of the market for corporate control. At the very least, the degree of contracting-out of counter services should be extended, perhaps by the sale of existing 'Crown' outlets.

The issue of privatising Royal Mail Letters remains a more thorny one in the absence of substantial competition and the continued existence of rather nebulous 'social obligations' requiring internal

---

[1] Corby, M. (1990): 'The Post Office: A Discussion Paper', London: Centre for Policy Studies.

funding. Until—as in New Zealand—these matters are resolved satisfactorily, it may be appropriate for letters to remain in the public sector. This would not rule out the possibility of a form of privatisation through the contracting-out of some of its activities. The Department of Trade and Industry reportedly[1] favours such an approach.

---

[1] 'DTI probe to help boost post office competition', *Financial Times*, 22 April 1991. (The Report has not yet been published.)

# THREE

# An Efficiency Analysis of the Effects of Greater Competition

The assumption in this section is that total *laissez-faire* is established in the British postal market, probably by unilateral action, but possibly via the European Commission conforming with the apparent dictate of the *Single European Act*. The consequences of complete competition are, of course, not totally clear, but a view of the consequences is presented in the first sub-section. A second sub-section examines what would happen in the unlikely event that *all* countries in the EC were simultaneously to remove their postal monopolies; it concentrates on the international implications of competition.

## 1. The Effects of Removing the UK Postal Monopoly

There has been a trend in the UK market, throughout the 1980s, towards increased competitiveness of postal services. Based on this experience with greater competition, experience elsewhere and theoretical considerations, I explore some of the possible implications of *complete* demonopolisation of the UK market. Other aspects are taken up in the next section. Whilst this analysis must be partly speculative, an increasingly clear picture is emerging of what would happen if competition were to be legalised completely.

The discussion initially revolves around a very simple model of the main postal markets, represented by Figure 1. Certain aspects of this model require further discussion and, perhaps, amendment. These aspects are discussed later, particularly in the following section on natural monopoly. Further, the model incorporates only static efficiency effects. Cost efficiency and dynamic efficiency are considered later.

### Letters

Competition will tend to have the greatest impact in local city markets where new entry will drive prices for some mail categories well below the existing Post Office rate of 22 pence for standard-size articles. I assume that the Post Office is able to vary its rates in response to competitive pressures. The available predictions and overseas evidence suggest a fall to about half the first-class rate as a consequence of local competition. I now consider some of this evidence. Exactly a century ago, Alfred Marshall (1891), a strong advocate of local competition, predicted that competition would drive the local price of a letter down from $1d$ to $1/2d$. This was based on empirical observation of the price charged by local services that were in the process of being closed down by the Post Office. Many of these services relied on an association with a local parcels service for their viability. More recently, the Post Office (1979) contemplated that next-day local delivery could occur at a rate of 6 pence, compared with the then first-class rate of 9 pence. This prediction seems to be too conservative. Even more recently, the Chairman of the Post Office has reportedly effectively predicted a competitive rate of 10 pence in the London area—less than half the existing Post Office rate.[1]

In Spain, the one country where competition at the local level is allowed (for certain business mail), the Correos charges 8 pesetas for local (i.e. intra-territorial) letters, compared with 20 pesetas for inter-territorial letters. Greater Madrid, for example, forms a territory. It is probably reasonable to assume that the rate charged by the Correos reflects the costs of, and therefore the price charged by, its competitors.

This assessment of the effect of local city competition implies the absence of significant *economies of scale\** in local delivery. More accurately, it implies that firms reach the minimum points of their long-run average cost curves at output levels well below market demand. This further implies that the area where people particularly worry about economies of scale—actual delivery—is not a significant concern. More than one post-person can ply the same route without significant cost disadvantage. I return to this question in the next section as part of the discussion of natural monopoly.

Another point worth making is that entrants will not necessarily compete on price and the Post Office will not necessarily react only with price changes. The free market will presumably throw up a

---

[1] Sir Bryan Nicholson is quoted in *The Economist* (15 December 1990) as saying that: 'Any fool could deliver for 10p in London.'

**Figure 1a**

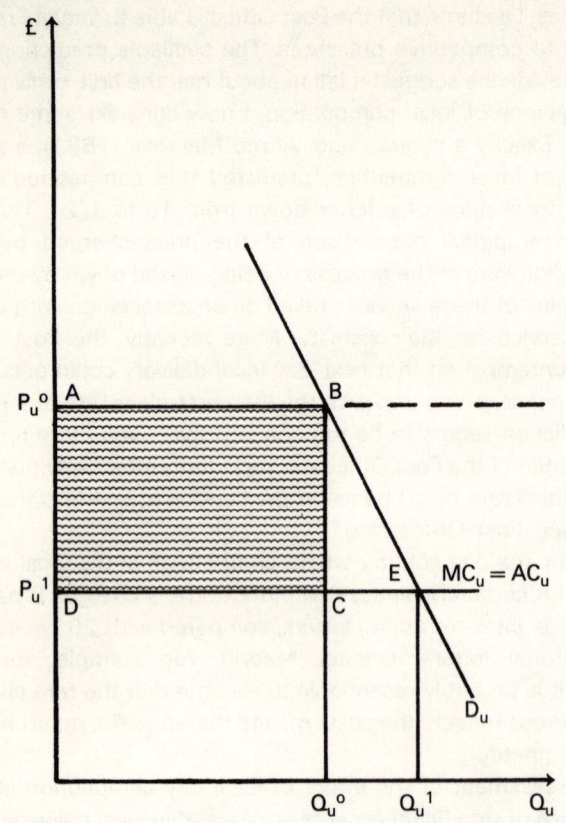

[Figure 1a: Graph with vertical axis £ and horizontal axis $Q_u$. Points $P_u^0$ and $P_u^1$ on vertical axis; $Q_u^0$ and $Q_u^1$ on horizontal axis. Rectangle ABCD shaded. Line $MC_u = AC_u$ horizontal through $P_u^1$, E. Demand curve $D_u$ downward sloping through B and E.]

range of service types, some more 'up-market' than the existing Post Office one, and some more 'standard'. Service speed, number of deliveries, delivery guarantees, etc., would be factors that vary in different offerings. As in other instances of deregulation (such as airlines in the United States) the market will give rise to some surprises.

In Figure 1a the initial 'monopoly' price on urban services is $P_u^0$ which generates a total 'surplus' of ABCD. Average cost ($AC_u$) and marginal cost ($MC_u$) are assumed equal at this stage.[1] The advent

---

[1] Estrin and de Meza, in a series of papers (e.g. 1991) analyse the effects of competition where there is a gap between average cost and marginal cost and where competition reduces the Post Office's volume. This raises its unit costs, so there is a negative externality on users of the Post Office service. This problem does not arise under the assumption in this section, but must be considered in the next section.

of competition forces the price down to average cost, eliminating the surplus but generating a gain to users of ABED. The net efficiency gain in this market segment is BEC (i.e. ABED minus ABCD).

In rural and some other household segments, the Post Office would probably continue to be the major carrier. These areas are serviced at a total *avoidable cost*\* which probably exceeds revenues generated, the resulting loss being made up by 'cross-subsidisation' from the surplus on urban services. The Post Office would no longer be able to cover the loss in this way, and in order to remain self-supporting, rural rates would have to rise sufficiently to cover costs. This rise could be quite substantial. Tabor (1987, p. 44) observed some years ago that

> 'before allocating overheads and profits, it costs about half as much again as the average to deliver a letter in a rural area. This would mean about 6p to 7p on a letter to the country'.

On present prices, this implies a rate of about 31 pence for rural letters.

As with those who enjoy a 'price reduction', those who suffer a 'price rise' may not do so in an explicit form. The 'quality' of service could be reduced instead. In particular, the second delivery could be a casualty for some users, and the delivery point may become more remote for people in rural areas. Reportedly, factors such as this have been considered in the Post Office Plan as part of a trade-off of service standards for willingness to take on more competition and to interconnect rivals.

These reductions in service quality would temper the explicit price increase. Furthermore, the rural 'price rise' could attract new entrants into providing rural services and these competitive pressures could help to keep costs and prices down. Some observers (e.g. Clarke, 1988) have expressed—with considerable persuasiveness—optimism about the prospects for rural postal users. The outlook for non-urban users in a competitive regime may not be as bleak as sometimes envisaged. We return to the possible problem of rural services in Section 5 on 'cross-subsidisation'. The rise in prices in the rural market will also result in an efficiency gain. As noted by Pryke (1981, p. 162):

> 'Charges would be raised for those postal activities where the price, *viz.* the value which marginal customers place on the service, is lower than the cost of provision. ... [Accordingly] the community would be

**Figure 1b**

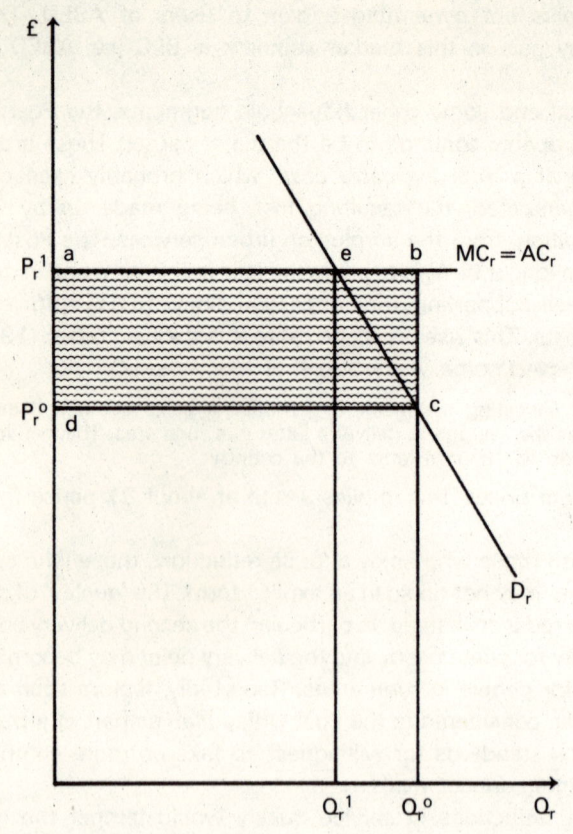

*[Figure 1b: Graph with £ on vertical axis and $Q_r$ on horizontal axis. Horizontal line $MC_r = AC_r$ at price $P_r^1$ with points a, e, b. Horizontal line at $P_r^0$ with points d, c. Demand curve $D_r$ slopes downward through e and c. Quantities $Q_r^1$ and $Q_r^0$ marked on horizontal axis.]*

better off because low value but high cost traffic ... would be discouraged.'

In Figure 1b price is initially at $P_r^0$ (equals $P_u^0$) and quantity is $Q_r^0$. With average cost of $AC_r$, there is a loss of abcd on rural activities, which is initially met by the surplus in the local city market. Breaking-even overall means that abcd must be equal to ABCD. Competition in the urban market must force the rural price up to cover costs overall. A rise in price to $P_r^1$ (equals $AC_r$) ends a 'loss' to the postal service of abcd and a loss to rural users of aecd, resulting in a net efficiency gain ebc (i.e. abcd minus aecd).

Another 'casualty' of competition could be the second-class service. Firm indications are that the difference in average avoidable cost between first- and second-class letters is less than 2 pence (see, e.g., Corby, 1990) in the face of a 5 pence price difference. This large price difference cannot successfully be given a *Ramsey-Boiteux price justification*\*, and one suspects that the cheap second-class service is run as a 'social service', under political pressure. The impact of competition on the first-class rate will force it down, plausibly making it difficult to sustain the second-class rate at its present level.

### Parcels and Premium Services

The markets for parcels, courier services, etc., have long been competitive and are presumably in long-run equilibrium with only normal profits. The gains from competition have already occurred, taking the form of price reductions and service improvements for existing products ('parcels') and the advent of new services ('premium' mail services). The allowance of competition in the other markets should not have any substantial impact in this market—price would remain at $P_c^o$ and quantity at $Q_c^o$ in Figure 1c. Thus, there are no efficiency implications.[1] However, if this market had been affected by predatory pricing by the official postal service, there would be an efficiency gain in this market as price would be forced up to 'true' unit cost.

When viewed in the context of this model, the effect of the introduction of complete competition is clear. Static efficiency effects are positive with total gains exceeding total losses by the areas BEC in Figure 1a and ebc in Figure 1b.[2]

### Cost Efficiency

I now consider the impact of competition on technical (or cost) efficiency. If the postal service had been provided at less than feasible technical efficiency, competitive pressures would force a more cost-efficient operation. This potential gain, which may be quite substantial, has been recognised by many observers over the years. For example, Rowland Hill,[3] a strong advocate of postal competition, expected that:

---

[1] There may be some substitutibility between the urban market and this courier market with the fall in $P_u$, resulting in a leftward shift in the 'courier' demand curve, $D_c$ (not shown). This would not affect efficiency.

[2] Gains and losses are added in unweighted terms—that is, the 'potential Pareto criterion' or 'pound-is-a-pound criterion' is used. This may offend the values of some observers.

[3] From Sir Rowland Hill and G. B. Hill, *The Life of Sir Rowland Hill and the History of the Penny Post* (1837), London: Frederick Warne, 1880, two vols.

**Figure 1c**

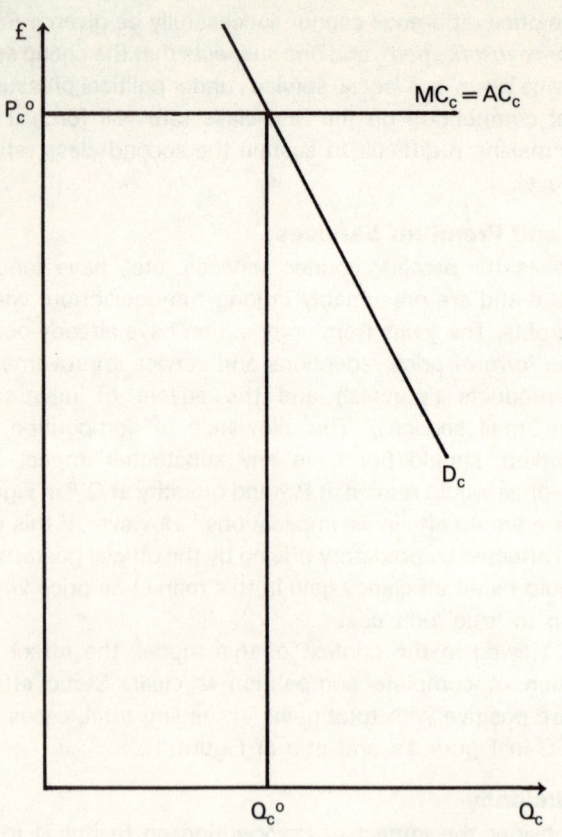

'[W]holesome competition [would occur] wherever the service is performed with less than the greatest efficiency and cheapness; a competition which ... would ... compel the department to have due regard to simple merit in its officers, and economic efficiency in all its arrangements.'

Ten years ago, Pryke (1981) drew attention to what he regarded as the 'ineptitude of PO management and the intransigence of postal workers ...' (p. 158). He concluded that the 'postal services are grossly inefficient', noting that 'costs are excessively large because far too many workers are employed'. Further, '[m]anagement has been inert and inept ...' (p. 161).

The 1980s was a decade of great improvement. My own assessment around the middle of the 1980s (Albon, 1987, p. 16) concluded that the Post Office 'has broadened its range of services, reduced its real unit costs, kept its charges in line with or below those prevailing overseas, and made a very handsome profit'.

The progress continued. Bishop and Kay (1988, p. 45) reported figures on growth of total factor productivity in the major public enterprises for the period 1979-88: the Post Office performed above the average. However, the rate of growth was lower for the latter part of the period. Further, Bishop and Kay attributed the Post Office's productivity growth more to

'a recovery from particularly lamentable performance during the 1970s than a great record of achievement' (pp. 43-44).

In spite of advances in the 1980s, there is almost certainly room for substantial further improvement. Estrin and de Meza (1990, p. 6) conclude that:

'[T]he performance of the Post Office has been improving somewhat since the late 1970s. However ... there is still room for the sort of efficiency improvements which might be expected ... from permitting competition.'

**Dynamic Efficiency**

There is the possibility of dynamic efficiency gains where competition finds new services and new methods. Historically, invention and innovation in postal services have come from the private sector. For example, the first 'penny post' was not an official invention. The service was first introduced in London in 1680 by William Docwra, who built up a substantial service based on a single price (1$d$) for local delivery. However, Docwra was not allowed by the Post Office to continue the service. It was taken over by the Post Office which continued to run it until the national penny post was introduced in 1840.

The 'Post Office' entry in the old *Palgrave's Dictionary* (*cf.* Higgs, 1926) gives other early British examples of private initiatives and notes that the Post Office 'at once encouraged, absorbed, and suppressed private enterprise' (p. 173). In the United States, the famous 'pony express' was not an official idea, but was commenced privately and taken over by the government service (*cf.* Haldi, 1974). More recently, private *courier*\* operations in many countries, including Britain, have opened up a new market segment with an emphasis on speed and delivery guarantees; they have been followed by the official postal service (e.g. Datapost in the UK,

Chronopost in France). The source of initiative is clear in all these cases.

**Combat Predation**

As we have already observed, competition can remove or substantially reduce the possibility of *'predatory pricing'**. Where an area is 'reserved' for the official carrier, this gives rise to the possibility of generating a 'fighting fund' to undercut rivals in competitive areas. The possibility of predatory pricing is a concern of the European Commission and has been the subject of litigation in Europe and elsewhere, especially the United States. It is a problem which can be attacked by releasing competitive forces.

## 2. The International Context

Suppose now that competition were introduced both within and between the various countries comprising the European Community, expanding the domain of private international carriers and opening up the possibility of real competition between the various official carriers. This would lead to the strong possibility of the various types of efficiency gains discussed in the previous subsection. In particular, pricing of international services would be forced to become more efficient and the least cost-efficient of the official post offices would be forced to raise their productivity under threat of losing business to private operators and other official services.

There is already a single market in intra-EC premium and parcel services, partly as a result of pressure from the European Commission on reluctant countries like Spain and Italy. Companies such as DHL, TNT and Federal Express, all with substantial European networks, have a major presence in the market. As mentioned above (p. 13), the official services have attempted to fight back by setting up a specialist international organisation, the IPC, with its trading arm, UNIPOST. The Chairman of this body, Gerard Harvey (1990, p. 9), has paid tribute to the innovative role of his private sector rivals, referring to their 'excellent proof of delivery' (p. 4), their structuring 'with the customer's interest [in] mind' (p. 7), and their providing the `template for success'. Essentially, the *'hub-and-spoke'** system was a private innovation in this area. The expansion of the private operators into other areas of postal services (e.g. intra-EC letter traffic) will bring benefits of innovation as well as placing pressure on inefficient pricing practices.[1]

Creation of an EC-wide single postal market for all items would also enhance the opportunities for official postal services to compete with each other. While their present relationship with each other tends to resemble that of a cartel, traditionally supported by the Universal Postal Union (UPU), there is already some competition between these services. In particular, differences between countries in rates for bulk mail have encouraged some users in more expensive countries to by-pass their own official services and to ship their mail to other less-expensive countries for on-mailing. The Netherlands postal service has emerged as a major hub for such mailings. Other forms of competition could also emerge in a liberalised market, although there may be a reluctance of the official services to abandon their co-operative arrangements and adopt a competitive one.

## Summary: the Benefits of EC-wide Competition

In summary, three types of benefit would be expected in the international arena from complete competition in the EC.

- Firstly, pricing would be forced to become more efficient. The move towards price uniformity throughout the EC (the first step being the agreement on letters from each member-state to other EC countries being charged at the member-state's inland rate) would be arrested, if not reversed, under competitive pressure. Various other pricing anomalies would also be threatened in a competitive environment.

- Secondly, there would be a tendency for inefficient official services to be by-passed as 'hubbing' became a more important structural characteristic. These official services would have to become more cost-efficient or lose much of their business. All the official services would have to improve their productivity, but this effect would be much stronger in the very inefficient countries such as Italy, Spain and Ireland, than in the UK and the Netherlands.

- Finally, new services and procedures would emerge, continuing a trend already established by the international couriers.

---

[1] The EC's Competition Commissioner, Sir Leon Brittan, has recently pledged that there will be complete freedom of all cross-border postal services ('Brittan pledges to bring competition to international postal services', *Financial Times*, 5 June 1991). This matter had been left open in the December 1990 'draft' of the *Green Paper*.

## FOUR

# Do Postal Services Constitute a Natural Monopoly?

Besides the expected benefits of competition, there are also possible costs. Traditionally, statutory monopoly in postal services has rested on two pillars: the alleged existence of *natural monopoly** and the support of cross-subsidisation within and across postal services. Not surprisingly, it is these two rationales that have been appealed to by the European Commission in its case for continued monopoly. Britain could undermine this argument by putting the natural monopoly to the market test, for if natural monopoly is not a serious problem in a national context it cannot be a problem in the broader European context.

### 1. Modification of the Model

Our analysis of competition in the previous section is based on the assumption that marginal cost and average cost are constant and the same. It was also assumed that there are no *economies of scope**. These are rather heroic assumptions and must be considered more carefully. The European Commission is particularly concerned about the coverage of fixed costs in a competitive environment, reflecting an underlying belief in *economies of scale**.

Suppose that there are economies of scale in each of the local city and rural markets, but not in the parcels and couriers markets. Figures 1a and 1b are no longer relevant and are replaced by Figures 2a and 2b. In each market there are separate overheads to be covered which raise average cost above marginal cost. The assumption of constant marginal costs, with $MC_r$ greater than $MC_u$, is retained. The Post Office is initially still constrained to set the same price in each market and does so in a manner which just results in covering all fixed and variable costs.[1] Again, the shaded

---

[1] If the postal service is constrained to a uniform price, it may not be able to choose the monopoly price, $P_u^o$, in the urban market as this may not be compatible with overall cost-recovery. A higher price may be necessary. Even though this lowers urban profits, choice of a higher price results in greater rural cost-recovery.

**Figure 2a**        **Figure 2b**

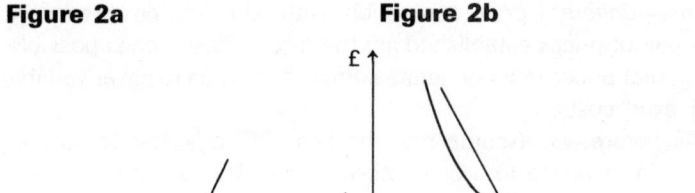

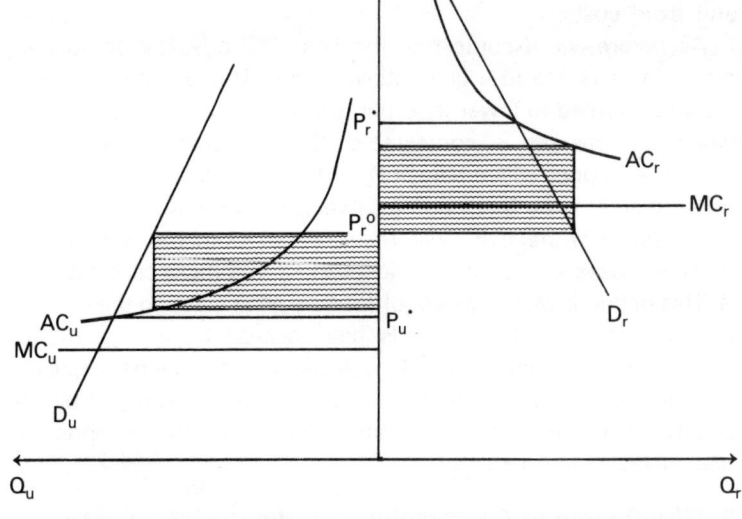

rectangle in the left-hand diagram has the same area as the shaded rectangle in the right-hand diagram. The price in the urban market is sufficient to cover overheads in the city market, overheads in the rural market and the rural deficit on variable costs.

Suppose now that entry was allowed into either or both markets. At the existing prices, no-one would be interested in entering the rural market where $AC_r$ is greater than $P_r^o$, but the urban market would be attractive if the Post Office retained its price at $P_u^o(=P_r^o)$. A new entrant could cover both overhead and variable costs at a price below the Post Office price. Such entry is often described as 'cream-skimming'.[1] If the urban price were forced down to the average cost level, $P_u^*$, there would be an efficiency gain in the urban market. Further, as funds are no longer available to fund the rural losses, there would have to be an increase in the Post Office's price in the rural market to $P_r^*$, which is the most efficient (i.e.

---

[1] The problem raised by Estrin and de Meza does not arise here because the Post Office does not lose any urban volume. Indeed, its urban volume increases. Where the market is fragmented, the Post Office will not necessarily lose volume either. This is because the whole market expands as a consequence of the lower price, and the Post Office could end up with a reduced market share of a larger total market in which its volume in fact increased.

*Ramsey-Boiteux**) price compatible with complete cost recovery. The pair of prices established are the most efficient ones possible, given that prices must generate sufficient revenue to cover variable and fixed costs.

As before, we assume that the Post Office is able to vary its prices in response to a competitive threat. The extent to which it would be forced to lower its urban price depends on the extent to which the market is contestable. If the market is not at all contestable, price will remain at $P_u^o(=P_r^o)$. If, on the other hand, the urban market is perfectly contestable, price will have to fall to $P_u^*$. Imperfect *contestability** will result in an outcome somewhere between these extremes, but closer to $P_u^*$ the more contestable it is. This depends on the extent of *sunk costs** in entering the market; whether or not potential rivals have access to state-of-the-art technology; the extent to which customers are tied (either legally or technically) to the incumbent; and the strategy employed by the incumbent to deter and/or thwart entrants. Are these conditions met in the postal industry?

## 2. The Degree of Contestability in the Postal Industry
### Sunk Costs

Sunk costs are the key item. According to Panzar (1991, p. 224), 'the postal network requires little in the way of [sunk costs]'. Mail services are labour and vehicle intensive and these costs do not constitute sunk costs. Other important facilities, such as premises for sorting and, where necessary, collection points can be leased, and do not require extensive dedicated equipment. Two areas, planning and advertising, do result in the incurring of irretrievable costs. However, if like Estrin and de Meza (1990) we place a lot of emphasis on these, we will be left wondering how any new businesses emerge in any industry. This question must also be considered in the light of the likely pattern of entry.

As noted previously, entry may come in the form of a large overall challenge by one of the national express carriers, such as that threatened in 1988 by TNT. This would be the case if a single additional national licence were issued by the Minister, but could also arise in a more liberal setting. TNT is already established in a closely related market and has a national capacity in that market. The big parcel and premium carriers have established customer bases and brand images. Television advertising has revealed their names, services and logos to the broader population. Their activity in the premium market has taught them the means of market entry and creation. They have experience in how official postal services react to rivalry. In most cases, the experience has been gained in more than one country, giving rise to knowledge of different types of obstacle and different counter-strategies. This background would be most valuable in expanding into higher-volume markets.

An alternative means of entry is that a number of firms enter local city markets—as many observers predict—possibly followed by a linkage of these local delivery services with a national 'premium' network (like DHL or TNT) for long-hauling of traffic. The Post Office (1979, para. 6.4) predicted that this 'might just reasonably create a seriously competitive equivalent to the first-class letter service'. The spread of local delivery services has been prevented by the £1 threshold. While a number have tried to come in at around the threshold (e.g. London Penny Post), they have failed because they have been too up-market to attract those who use the ordinary letter services, and too down-market for existing premium users. Removing the threshold—or even lowering it to, say, 40 pence—would give this new market a significant chance of success.

Of course, as in the past, the market may surprise everybody in the way it spurns competition. Indeed, it is this element of surprise which makes *complete* opening of the market so attractive. Only in circumstances where new entrants have the unfettered opportunity to offer new services and try new processes can the gains of dynamic efficiency be fully realised. This is just one reason for rejecting the limited licensing approach advocated by the Adam Smith Institute (1991) and premium companies like TNT.

**Customer Tieing**

Customer-tieing to the incumbent is probably not a major consideration. There is no physical tie (as in telecommunications) and there is no obvious legal tie. However, the Post Office will attempt to do deals with larger customers based on their total loyalty to the traditional supplier. There is already some evidence of this in the UK and, notably, in New Zealand where, as observed by Toime (1991, p. 281):

> 'New Zealand Post's ability to put an integrated proposal together, based on interdependent pricing, is a considerable strength.'

**Access to Technology**

Access to technology is not a problem in the postal industry. If a new operation were to seek to install, say, state-of-the-art Optical Character Recognition (OCR) sorting equipment, there appears to be no reason why they could not purchase it. No postal administration holds patents on this equipment. Perhaps more importantly, most of the equipment required for postal operation is neither dedicated nor sophisticated.

**Anti-Competitive Strategies**

Finally, it is difficult to see how an incumbent postal service could engage in anti-competitive strategies where the province of the free market is complete. Only where the market is partially opened can the incumbent engage in predatory practices since, firstly, profits from 'reserved' areas may be generated, and, secondly, exposure to competition is limited. Where there are no reserved services, competitive pressures in *all* markets will make it impossible for the incumbent to generate funds to fight price-wars or to fight off all competitive threats.

**A Market Test?**

These considerations lead to the conclusion that there is a strong case for the market test, even if we think there are economies of scale. This is because the market appears quite contestable. The expectation must be one of opening the market, leading to the various benefits of competition with little expected cost if new ventures fail. The potential gains from efficient pricing, cost efficiency and innovation appear much greater (and more likely) than any potential costs.

## 3. The Empirical Evidence on Overall Economies of Scale

Are economies of scale, in practice, important in local postal services? This question has been examined by many observers in the UK, including Senior (1970 and 1989), Albon (1987), Pryke (1981), Estrin and de Meza (1990 and 1991), Jones (1991), the Post Office (1979), Tabor (1991), and Dobbs and Richards (1991). Assessments of the extent of overall economies of scale vary. Consider, for example, the verdict of Pryke (pp. 161-62). He concludes that if 'there were several rival concerns operating over the same ground it is doubtful whether delivery costs would be very much inflated. ... [A] fall in the volume of traffic ought to be largely matched by a reduction in expenditure'.

Estrin and de Meza reach a rather different conclusion about the entire postal service. Based on data for the period 1971 to 1988, they find that a 10 per cent increase in output would raise costs by only about 6 per cent, indicating 'strongly increasing returns to scale' (1990, p. 4). There are many problems with such aggregate studies. For example, there have been considerable advances in technology over this period, so one has to ask whether the researchers are picking up real economies of scale or the outcome of a shifting cost function giving the appearance of scale economies. In this particular case there is a crude attempt to account for technological change, but there is a more fatal flaw.

Estrin and de Meza's result would be more convincing if the data period had been one of consistently increasing output. The first several years of their sample period were ones of decreasing output but not decreasing staff. The tenure-ridden and slow-moving Post Office could not (and probably would not) shed staff in response to the fall in output. The observations for the 1970s will thus show a small or even zero elasticity of cost to output, but this certainly does not reflect underlying economies of scale. When output again began to grow in the 1980s, the Post Office did not need to, and was effectively constrained not to, increase its staffing. Output grew by using up excess labour supplies at hand. Again, economies of scale are not indicated. This pattern of output and labour usage is clear from Estrin and de Meza's graph of labour productivity (1990, Figure 2), which falls until about 1977, levels out for a few years and then begins to rise in 1981.

The evidence in other countries is also, at best, lukewarm about the presence of economies of scale in postal services. Consider, for example, Roger Sherman's (1989) book on *The Regulation of Monopoly* in which he reviews the evidence of economies of scale in the United States Postal Service. The evidence does not support the existence of significant economies of scale. One study found that, in larger regional offices, there were diseconomies of scale. Sherman reports that 'in its own statistical study the Post Office ... found no evidence of economies of scale' (p. 266). Sherman also notes, with examples, that 'Accounting methods ... were biased toward making economies of scale ... appear greater than they really were. ...' (p. 266).

The conclusion on economies of scale is somewhat uncertain in that there is some evidence that aggregate postal costs rise less fast than output but that this result is not decisive. Even if it were, it does not appear to matter very much. The postal industry is comprised of a number of services, each with a number of distinct phases—collection, sorting, transport and delivery. Knowledge of the industry will be advanced more by a detailed disaggregative approach than through a rather futile search for the existence or not of aggregate 'economies of scale'.

## 4. A Disaggregative Approach to Economies of Scale

An evaluation of the extent of 'natural monopoly' requires a disaggregated study. Tabor (1991) has organised his thoughts on this question in a useful Table (Table 1). Arrows in the Table represent transportation.

It is convenient to revolve the discussion around the stages in Table 1—collection, sorting, transport and delivery.

### Collection

Collection has perhaps 'moderate' economies of scale but will not be a problem for the most likely type of entry envisaged. For example, companies specialising in bulk mailings (for instance, gas and electricity bills, bank statements, company annual reports, and so on) will not have a collection problem, being able to collect the items directly from the mailer. In this circumstance, sorting would also not pose a difficulty as the items would be pre-sorted. In other cases, where dispersed collection and sorting are required, entry will be more difficult. It will be interesting to see how these problems are tackled. One possibility for collection would be to 'piggy-back' on existing pick-up services such as those for film developing and processing. More likely will be the development of collection boxes in safe places such as service stations, building foyers, and the like.

### Sorting

Sorting, which will be required only for dispersed mail collections, will require reasonably large facilities handling quite high volumes. However, huge volumes are not obviously necessary. For example,

## Table 1:
## The Letter Process

| Process: | Collection | → | Outward Sorting (Office of Origin) | → | Intermediate Sorting | → | Inward Sorting (Distant Sorting Centre) | → | Preparation/Delivery (Office of Destination) |
|---|---|---|---|---|---|---|---|---|---|
|  |  |  | 25% |  |  |  | 75% |  |  |
| *Cost:* | Moderate |  | Low |  | Low |  | Low |  | High |
| *Degree of Scale Economies:* |  |  |  |  |  |  |  |  |  |

*Source:* Tabor, 1991, p. 35.

Royal Mail Letters has more than 50 major sorting facilities—hardly indicative of serious economies of scale. Australia Post has seven mail exchanges in Sydney alone, a city of less than four million people. The experience has been one where many of the world's postal services flirted with centralisation of sorting but soon found that this produced diseconomies of scale. This led to a reversion to decentralisation. If there do prove to be difficulties with sorting costs, this could lead to the development of specialised sorting companies, handling mail for more than one mailing company. Another possibility is that the official service could take in sorting work for private operators, perhaps at off-peak times when, at least in Britain, there is growing excess capacity.

## Transport

Transport will not be a problem for local delivery companies. However, if such operators wish to offer a broader service they will require long-haul transport. This may be handled directly by the operator, but is more likely to involve interconnection with another (or other) carrier(s). As with all such decisions the best choices are likely to be made by private firms with a strong pecuniary interest in the outcome.

## Delivery

Delivery is the stage assessed by Tabor as having 'high' economies of scale. It is also an area accounting for a significant proportion (perhaps a third) of total postal costs. Dobbs and Richards (1991, pp. 85-86) and other critics of postal competition often ridicule the idea of more than one post-person visiting the same premises. Of course, in some countries, the post-person makes two daily deliveries, leading to some *prima facie* doubt about the extent of economies of scale. This doubt is heightened when it is considered how many others make separate delivery visits—at least one newspaper delivery, handbill distributors, one or more milk vendors.[1] Why aren't these deliveries consolidated if there are economies to be gained? If delivery proves to be a problem, there is the possibility that specialised delivery companies could be developed to distribute the mail of more than one mailing company.

---

[1] In New Zealand, the milk vendors already deliver 'circulars'. Their service, Homelink, claims it could provide a uniform postal service at a lower price than New Zealand Post (*cf.* Prebble, 1989, p. 14).

It is easy to imagine former post office staff establishing such services, drawing on their specialised local knowledge of such operations.

Yet another approach to delivery is *interconnection** with the official postal service for delivery. In those countries which have significantly deregulated telecommunications, it has been recognised that local distribution poses a particular problem to new entrants. This has been handled by providing interconnection rights to alternative suppliers on an 'equal access' basis. In the United States, for example, various competing long-distance operators carry traffic which usually gets to and from their networks through the agency of the local 'Bell' operating companies. The price and conditions of access are the same as those for the 'incumbent', AT+T. This system appears to work very well, although the tendency is towards 'by-pass' of the local companies (*cf.* Beesley and Laidlaw, 1989, pp. 47-49).[1]

In the postal area, interconnection poses problems that are not present (or not as severe) in telecommunications. In particular, quality of service and service guarantees would be difficult in the absence of providing a complete end-to-end service. For example, there have been reports of difficulties when 'private mail' enters the public system as *remail** in one or two of the continental EC countries. Even the official postal services have difficulties with interconnection in some countries. For example, mail to Italy and Spain is often difficult for the British Post Office. In the same vein, problems of interconnection have led Parcelforce to separate itself almost completely from Royal Mail Letters. This case is considered in the next sub-section.

## 5. Economies of Scope in the Postal Industry

Another possible basis for natural monopoly is the existence of 'economies of scope' where there are gains in the form of a lower total cost of having a single firm supplying the different services. For the case of two services, q1 and q2, the cost function is such that:

$$C(q1, q2) < C(q1, 0) + C(0, q2).$$

[1] By-pass occurs largely because interconnection is charged at too high a price. This, in turn, largely arises because local usage prices are regulated to ridiculously low levels, and the regional operating companies must be allowed large access charges to remain viable.

We need to determine whether, in particular, it is more economical to have the Post Office operate both the letters and parcels/premium services and whether or not there are any gains from joint operation of both city and rural letter services.

At least in the case of parcels and *express mail**, there do not appear to be any advantages of joint operation with letters. The trend has been firmly towards separation of these services within the official service. In the case of the UK, 'Parcelforce' is now a quite distinct business from Royal Mail 'Letters'. The parcels division of the Post Office was created as a separate business in 1986 and has since developed almost totally independently of the other Post Office divisions. It now has its own network of totally independent sorting, transport and local delivery depots. The Managing Director of Parcelforce, Nick Nelson (1990), has said that this separation arose because

> 'the Post Office understood that parcel activity was different from the normally understood perception of postal activity ...' (p. 3).

Nelson even remarks that 'I know it sounds incongruous, but ... I cannot allow myself to think in postal terms' (p. 8). Similar splits have occurred—or are in process—in other postal services.

The very success of private parcel and courier operations is further evidence of the absence of economies of scope. These services have flourished without an association with a letter service or an established counter operation. Further, they have been subject, in some cases, to predatory pricing, and have nonetheless succeeded. It is now the case that within the UK there are several complete parcel/premium mail networks which operate side-by-side in competition with each other. Even if there is a significant 'shake-out' in the market, the development in recent years clearly shows that there are no economies of scope between letter services and parcels/courier services. It also clearly shows that any economies of scale in parcels and courier operations are exhausted at output levels which are small relative to total market size. Further, while this is true within the UK, it is also true of the EC market as as whole. As noted in Section 3, there are now several separate European networks, including that constructed by the official post offices (UNIPOST) and those of DHL, TNT and Federal Express. Again, economies neither of scope nor of scale are indicated.

## 6. Is Natural Monopoly an Obstacle to Postal Competition?

Natural monopoly, in the form of either economies of scale or of scope, may form the basis of an argument against competition. The authors of the draft sections of the *Green Paper* have appealed to such an argument in their concern about fixed costs being covered in a competitive regime. In particular, they point to economies of scale, rather than economies of joint production. However, I have to consider both possibilities.

### Economies of Scale

There is some evidence of overall economies in the UK. This evidence is rather weak and, most importantly, even if there are such economies, the issue then becomes one of whether or not the market is contestable. Here the evidence suggests that the market is significantly contestable. For example, Panzar (1991), who does regard the postal service as a natural monopoly, claims that this 'in no way exempts the industry from competitive reform' (p. 219). Furthermore, the

> 'network structure of postal service and the relative lack of sunk costs convince me that competition can be more aggressively injected into postal service' (p. 225).

In those areas where competition has been permitted, the market appears to be highly contestable, if not 'competitive'. Detailed investigation of the experience with competition so far, and consideration of the degree of contestability of areas that are presently reserved, suggests a sanguine outlook for competitive domestic and international markets in the EC. Significant benefits of static, technical and dynamic efficiency will result if successful entry does occur.

Of course, this does not necessarily mean that the further extension of competition would not uncover the existence of economies of scale or scope within the letter service itself. This would be advantageous to the incumbent operator and could mean that new entrants would fail. This could entail some waste. However, the success of competition so far makes this outcome unlikely. Again, the benefits of allowing competition are likely to be large and quite probable; the costs quite small and unlikely. Accordingly, the expected pay-off is positive, and the market test is worth undertaking.

# FIVE

# Continued Cross-Subsidisation as a Basis for Statutory Monopoly

In addition to natural monopoly, the 'internal' support of universal service at a *uniform price\** is often appealed to as a basis for the statutory monopoly. At present Britain, like all the EC countries, practices some sort of *cross-subsidisation\**. The particular concern is with those services that do not even cover direct costs at their existing prices, and are supported by implicit taxes in other areas protected by statutory monopoly. Servicing rural areas at a uniform geographical price is the principal example. As we saw in Section 3, the advent of successful competition would reduce or eliminate the ability to cross-subsidise. What are the options on this front?

## 1. Letting Prices Adjust

One possibility is simply to let prices adjust to competition. As argued earlier, this would tend to enhance economic efficiency in the situation where the value of these subsidies to their recipients is less than the cost of their provision. There may also be dynamic efficiency gains as well. Competition would open up these subsidised markets to the possibility of new entrants who are more cost-efficient and/or who offer different types of service. As has so often happened historically, private initiatives could lead to socially beneficial invention and innovation in the provision of rural and other non-business postal services.

Some will argue that this *laissez-faire* approach is, in some sense, 'unfair'. Subjective valuations of this kind are not really the province of the economist. However, it may be observed logically that if existing subsidies are regarded as being 'fair', then, implicitly, the existing taxes on some users must also be viewed as being 'fair'. That is, supporters of this arrangement on 'equity' grounds must regard the whole structure as 'fair'. If recipients are favoured and payers are disfavoured, it is reasonable to expect that there is some independent attribute of worthiness of one group that is not possessed by the other. Where the difficulty lies is in trying to identify that attribute. The only obvious distinguishing feature is that one group receives and the other pays, but to identify this as the distinctive attribute would be tautological.

In spite of its adverse efficiency implications and its dubious claims to 'fairness', 'cross-subsidisation' has a significant degree of support, and not only from the recipients. If subsidies are to be retained in the system, the question arises as to whether these are best financed from implicit or explicit taxation and, if the latter, what is the best form of direct support. Consideration of these questions has a long history. We treat each aspect in turn.

## 2. Direct Subsidies from Explicit Taxes?

Disillusionment with implicit taxes and subsidies goes back a long way, at least to the father of the penny post. It is interesting to recall that Rowland Hill was not a supporter of cross-subsidisation. This has been revealed strongly by Coase (1939), Daunton (1985), Senior (1989) and others. Hill only supported a uniform price for the *'primary distribution*'*, within and between *post towns**. This was based on the near-uniformity of costs for such services which had been carefully estimated by Hill. For the *'secondary distribution*'*, Hill advocated that the service be charged at its direct cost.[1]

Hill also raised the possibility of *local funding* of subsidies to local postal services. If the local authority so desired, it could operate the local service itself, using either direct charges or parish rates to finance it. In a similar spirit, the local authority could subsidise the Post Office to operate the service in the locality at the uniform rate. Reluctantly, and later to his regret, Hill instead promoted the complete 'penny post' in order to achieve political acceptability. Hill's approach has many attractions, both as a solution within a particular country and for the EC as a whole.

Alternatively, subsidies could be *nationally funded*, or, in the EC

---

[1] There was a somewhat 'modern' flavour to Hill's proposal in that he advocated extension of services at what would now be called 'subsidy-free prices', just covering 'incremental cost' (i.e., 'without *injury* to [net] revenue'), and was prepared to recoup fixed costs from the primary distribution. Brown and Sibley (1986, pp. 51-58) explain these modern terms, and the relevant quotations from Hill's *Life* are set out in Coase (1939, pp. 428-29). Hill referred to recoupment of fixed costs as 'taxation'.

context, funded from Brussels. Central funding has been adopted in New Zealand for the support of local post offices. An amount of $NZ42 million was provided for this purpose in the first year after corporatisation, but counter service has since been rationalised by closures and substitution of more suitable arrangements. The draft of the EC's *Green Paper* considers the possibility of supporting postal services in some 'depressed areas' through direct subsidies.

One important question is whether the efficiency cost of paying for subsidies through open taxation falls short of or exceeds the efficiency cost of the existing system of covert taxes. This is an empirical question with the answer depending primarily on the own-price elasticity of demand for letters (determining the 'severity' of the covert tax on postal users) and the elasticity of supply of labour (determining the 'severity' of the income tax). In the case of Japan (*cf.* Albon, 1990), there is no contest—the income tax is a much more efficient way of raising revenue than the letter tax. This is also true, although less dramatically, of Australia (Albon, 1991a). It would be of some interest to pursue this empirical question for the UK and other European countries.

Of course, this is not the only efficiency question. Use of the covert tax method results in a direct efficiency cost (through inefficient pricing) but it also robs society of the other benefits of competition—greater cost efficiency, new services and new procedures. The issue of direct versus indirect costs is, therefore, much broader than that discussed in the previous paragraph.

Another advantage of direct subsidisation is its *transparency* compared with cross-subsidisation. Whereas a subsidy in the form of a price lower than avoidable cost and financed by over-charging other users is hidden from public scrutiny, a direct subsidy financed by general taxes is open to public appraisal and review. For example, the cost of support of rural counter services in New Zealand became obvious after corporatisation and the introduction of an explicit subsidy. Similarly, in Canada, certain services (e.g. newspapers, periodicals and books, parliamentary mail, and transport of foodstuffs to native communities) now receive direct support for their subsidy element.

## 3. The Mechanics of Direct Support

There are various possible means of ensuring universal service at a 'standard' rate. In a competitive environment, the best way to organise servicing of remote areas could be a matter for local decision, reflecting the particular circumstances. One possibility would be for a national approach to the 'secondary distribution' where it is is divided into franchise areas. The franchises to service the basic postal requirements of these areas could be auctioned on the basis of the subsidy required by the potential operator to service the area fully under specified conditions and at specified rates. The operator requiring the least subsidy would attain the contract for a specified period. It is even possible that the 'subsidy' could be negative. This has been argued by Clarke (1988) in the UK context and by Prebble (1989) for New Zealand.

Various groups might tender for available franchises. It would have to be decided whether the Post Office itself would be allowed to tender. An obvious source of tenders would be from associations of sub-postmasters in particular geographical areas. The sub-postmasters have significant local knowledge and an established presence in the postal industry. Another source of tenders could be former Post Office employees having local knowledge and experience in the industry. Thirdly, established courier companies, large and small, might be interested in servicing particular markets. Of course, other companies might be formed specifically to seek this kind of work.

At least in the initial stages, operation of such a scheme would probably require the possibility of guaranteed interconnection with the official post office, with conditions of entry into the official network regulated, either under general competition law or by a specific regulatory body.

## 4. The Way Forward

It is vitally important not to fall into the trap of accepting the manifest and large costs of monopoly in order to preserve implicit subsidies. It has been very convenient for national governments to maintain covert political favours at a small *per capita* cost to the majority of postal users. The political mechanism has allowed this to occur because the political clout of the well-organised recipients has outweighed that of the payers, who are relatively weak because of their large number and small individual interests. Given its dubious 'fairness' and its obvious inefficiency, government has strong domestic reasons to demonopolise and deregulate. There is now a broader argument in favour of allowing competition, perhaps with explicit subsidies. Under the plans of the European Commission the implicit tax-to-subsidy flows could become international. For example, British postal users could end up supporting low prices in countries with relatively inefficient postal services if the EC takes control of postal regulation and proceeds towards an EC Federal Post Office and a Community-wide uniform price for reserved services.

It is useful to pause and consider the implications of a uniform price for letters across the EC, assuming that the Commission has some means of effecting a cross-subsidy. If so, a rough idea of the uniform price compatible with the existing extent of overall cost-recovery can be determined by calculating the weighted average of existing basic letter rates in the 12 countries. All of the larger countries have higher rates than Britain's weighted average of the first- and second-class rates (weighted by volumes), which is currently 20 pence. In France the basic rate is 23 pence, in Germany 30 pence, and in Italy 30 pence. A rough weighted average is 25 pence. This means British users would pay 5 pence more to send a domestic letter, representing a massive implicit tax of about £750 million a year. This amount would be transferred to protect the existing inefficiencies of other European postal services and to lower the price to users in the more expensive countries like Italy and Germany. Of course, *this tax would be lower if the Commission could find a way of making the high-cost postal services more efficient. Short of a strong injection of competition, there does not appear to be any easy way of achieving this result.*

What is important is that the European Commission clearly intends to move towards uniformity. This will make pricing more inefficient and will cement in place national monopolies on basic services. Rather than centralisation, the tendency should be towards localisation, with individual member-countries—and perhaps regions within them—having responsibility for decisions about whether to subsidise and, if so, through what form. In this way the questions of monopolisation and subsidisation can be clearly separated, allowing postal users to benefit from competition.

## SIX

# Policy Options in Britain

The European Commission's exercise of preparing the *Green Paper* appears to represent an attempt to lock-in the member-countries of the EC to an anti-competitive policy stance to support harmonisation. This will be both inefficient and detrimental to Britain's interests. While there is some attempt at a compromise (for example, regulation would be set at the most liberal existing level), the Commission is obviously attempting to make postal services an exception to the free trade in goods and services that should mark Europe after 1992. There is no obvious 'legal' basis for doing this and, as has been argued in the two previous sections, there is no clear economic rationale for adopting this stance. Given that there is no legal basis for the continued monopolisation of postal services, Britain still has a chance to adopt an independent policy. That is, even if the rest of the EC wants to retain monopoly structures, Britain can demonopolise. Not only would such a course be possible; it would also be desirable for both domestic and strategic reasons.

### 1. The Implications of Different Possible Outcomes

The most efficient outcome for Europe as a whole would be one where all countries adopted a competitive stance and where each country made individual decisions on whether to replace cross-subsidies with direct subsidies to users in remote areas. Such an outcome would also be the best possible one for the UK, which would gain from both the introduction of competition and also from the market opportunities that would become available for the British Post Office.

Static and dynamic efficiency gains are likely to flow from demonopolisation. Britain would enjoy these benefits irrespective of the stance taken in the rest of the EC. However, there are other possible gains to Britain if there was total demonopolisation. These arise because the British Post Office is in a better position to gain business in other member-countries than are their postal services to gain business elsewhere. That is, *the British Post Office could reap considerable returns by expanding into Europe.*

The pay-off matrix (with ++ for the benefits of competition to users and + for the benefits of entry to a carrier) could look something like this:

**Demonopolisation in Rest of Europe**

|  |  | No | Yes |
|---|---|---|---|
| Demonopolisation in UK | No | 0,0 | +,++ |
|  | Yes | ++,+ | +++,++ |

[Britain's pay-off on the left; the rest of Europe on the right, in each cell.]

Suppose then that demonopolisation occurred throughout the EC (lower right cell). In addition to the efficiency gains already considered, Britain would gain because its Post Office is much better placed than most to gain business in other countries. It is probably the leanest and most cost-efficient postal service in Europe with the greatest experience in the market. Consider these facts about the British Post Office.

o Firstly, unlike some of its sister organisations, it is totally separate from telecommunications operations which has precluded the possibility of telecommunications profits supporting postal losses. Furthermore, of those that are split, Britain's has been split the longest.

o Secondly, the British Post Office has more market exposure than any other in the EC, with the private threshold set at the equal lowest weight (500g) and the lowest price (£1).

o Thirdly, in spite of having the lowest (or amongst the lowest) letter rates, it has consistently made profits since the late 1970s and is the only one to do so.

So, in these respects, and compared with its potential rivals, the Royal Mail is poised to do well in a liberalised market. At least in the short term—that is, until the others lift their games—the British Post Office (and, thus, Britain as a whole) would benefit from complete liberalisation in Europe. This would imply the desirability of rejecting the likely message of the *Green Paper* and argument to the Commission, on both economic and legal grounds, in favour of an open market. Securing of this outcome would result in the maximum possible gains for Britain (+++).

At the very least, the UK should insist on the deregulation of intra-Community and international mail services, which currently constitute about 4 per cent of total postal services. This would mean that carriers in any member-country could collect and deliver items bound from and to any other member-country. Such services would become 'fifth freedom' rights, protected by the doctrine of free trade among members enshrined in the *Single European Act*. This outcome, at least, now seems likely.

Suppose that the British Government failed in its bid to get demonopolisation throughout the EC. Would it still be desirable for Britain to remove its own monopoly? One concern might be that the various other European postal services (such as Dutch Post, France's *La Poste* and the Belgian Post Office) would enter the UK market without the Royal Mail having reciprocal rights to enter their markets. With only one minor caveat, this outcome is good for the UK (++) but not as good as complete liberalisation. There would still be benefits to British postal users, and these would exceed the losses to the Post Office. However, there would be no gains to the Post Office from expanded business opportunities.

One possible concern is that national carriers entering the market may not observe the 'rules of the game', and practice predatory pricing. Private competitors have neither the ability nor the incentive to engage in 'predatory' practices by supporting competitive operations from monopoly profits. This may not be true of some of Europe's government-owned operations, which have not yet been developed along business lines. Success may not be measured in terms of profits (or may be incorrectly measured), perhaps leading to unprofitable market entry. However, this will be of benefit to British postal users, over-and-above the normal benefits from competition. Furthermore, the costs of the subsidy will be borne outside Britain. There may be costs to Britain if the predation drove British suppliers out of business and if those casualties had incurred sunk costs. However, I have argued in Section 4 that sunk costs do not appear to be particularly important, especially in those types of operation where entry is likely.

## 2. Is More Competition Inevitable?

To some extent, the decision will be taken out of the hands of governments at national and European levels. Competition has a certain inevitability about it. In all nations in the EC the old monopoly structures have been broken down to a greater or lesser extent. Even those countries, like Italy, that have resisted, have been forced by the European Commission to begin deregulation. Some, like the UK and the Netherlands, have gone a long way. Express mail and parcel services are now not only competitive within countries, but also between them. Indeed, the international arena is that in which the couriers and parcel carriers have excelled, forcing the official services to retaliate by setting up the IPC. Of course, the IPC is copying the private operators. According to its President (Harvey, 1990, p. 9):

> 'The template for success ... [is] to reorganise along the lines of our competitors ..., separating out international divisions ... and moulding them into a truly multinational type organisation.'

Total private courier business is estimated by the Association of European Express Carriers at nearly £11 billion a year,[1] and this is a rapidly growing area. In addition to private competition, the national carriers are also beginning to compete with each other. For example, the Netherlands postal service is developing as a hub for bulk mailings. Some of the others are tending to try and maintain the cartel, but this will be difficult without government support.

Accordingly, the European Commission may not be able to ensure the retention of national postal monopolies, even if all countries supported its approach. There has been significant private competition as well as some 'competition' between countries, in spite of the existing regulations. The *Green Paper* promises some freeing of the market, and it is difficult to see that this will not promote more competition between countries. Once this begins to occur, the whole 'cartel' could break down. As the UK Government has observed in regard to telecommunications, '... regulation which inhibits telecommunications development will ... be increasingly difficult to enforce'.[2] This is also true of postal

---

[1] Quoted in 'Couriers give stamp of disapproval to postal blueprint', *Financial Times*, 10 December 1990.

[2] Department of Trade and Industry (1990), para. 4.22.

services where regulations have become difficult to enforce within countries, and it will become increasingly difficult to restrict competition between countries. Will the European government be strong enough to prevent competition from breaking out?

## SEVEN

# Conclusion

The 1992 phenomenon presents a strong opportunity—and an obligation—to introduce competition in postal services in Europe. The potential economic benefits from a true single market seem substantial and the possible costs appear both unlikely and relatively small. Any case against putting 'natural monopoly' or the degree of contestability to the market test is extremely weak. Subsidies to rural users can be accommodated in more open and (probably) more efficient ways than at present, and do not constitute a credible reason for preserving statutory monopoly. However, the indications are that the European Commission's *Green Paper* will not endorse major demonopolisation, although it would force the more restrictive national services to fall into line with the most liberal ones, and it would even-up the playing-field in other ways. It will almost certainly recommend the freeing of intra-EC mail. But this approach is far too cautious.

Britain's postal industry is both the most liberal and the most efficient in the EC. These two facts are, of course, not unrelated, and it is a credit to some farsighted politicians of the past that such a liberal policy was adopted. However, Britain could benefit by further freeing of the market—there is still a lot of room for improvement in all aspects of efficiency. In spite of this, successive Secretaries of State over nearly a decade have failed to demonopolise further, even where they have obvious sympathies with freer markets.

One reason for inaction has been a fear of the electoral repercussions of the possibility of higher prices and/or lower service in some rural areas. However, competition is not a zero-sum game—the benefits will outweigh the losses allowing for the possibility of compensation of the losers. Various mechanisms of compensation are possible and, in this context, there is less excuse to shy away from a more liberal policy. Making rural subsidies more explicit would be a desirable step irrespective of whether artificial entry barriers were removed or not.

The *Single European Act* of 1987 should have been the cue for Britain to move to greater liberalisation, both for its own sake and to give the rest of the EC a strong prod towards reducing market closure. Instead, officialdom in the UK has been indifferent to, or has even condoned, the emphasis of the European Commission on 'harmonisation' rather than its clear duty to promote competition. There is still time for Britain to force the issue by liberalising its own market and insisting that the Commission pursue its proper charter on the single market. This cannot entail the continuation of restrictions on intra-EC mail or, in the slightly longer term, the maintenance of national monopolies.

Harmonisation can only harm Britain. It will mean the cementing in place of significant monopoly powers in order to support gross inefficiencies of official operations in some member-states and, ultimately, it will probably result in an EC-wide uniform letter price. This will cost British users hundreds of millions of pounds annually—perhaps about 4 pence per letter in current values. This will be in addition to the losses from not having the more efficient postal industry that would be delivered by greater competition. In contrast, ossification of statutory monopoly could lead to a lapse in the Royal Mail's exemplary performance.

# Glossary

***Avoidable Costs:*** The cost-savings—both current and capital—that would result if a particular service were completely withdrawn.

***Contestability:*** A market where the absence of SUNK COSTS, access to production technology and to customers allows a potential entrant the possibility of entry without substantial loss if unsuccessful. A NATURAL MONOPOLY may be forced to efficient RAMSEY-BOITEUX PRICING if the market is contestable. (*See* Waterson, 1988, pp. 28-34; Sherman, 1989, pp. 77-87; and Berg and Tschirhart, 1988, pp. 30-34, 341-43, for useful and up-to-date summaries.)

***Courier:*** A mail carrier where the item carried is collected from the sender directly and delivered directly to the recipient.

***Cross-Subsidy:*** A situation where some users or usages are charged below AVOIDABLE COSTS while others are charged above avoidable costs in a manner such that overall costs are covered.

***Economies of Scale:*** A situation where the average cost of producing an item falls as the amount of it produced increases.

***Economies of Scope:*** A situation where given amounts of two or more services can be produced together at a lower total cost than if produced in separate production processes.

***Express Mail:*** Mail which is carried at a more rapid rate than the standard mail service with guaranteed delivery in the advertised time; sometimes called TIME-SENSITIVE MAIL.

***Hub-and-Spoke Distribution:*** A system of distribution where mail is collected in the various areas, transported along 'spokes' to a centralised sorting facility ('hub'), and then sent back out along the spokes for delivery.

***Interconnection:*** Where a service-provider uses part of the network of another service-provider (usually the former statutory monopolist) to provide its service. Conditions and prices of access to the network may have to be regulated, perhaps by a specific regulatory body.

*Letter:* The legal definition varies from country to country but it usually involves a written communication, physically carried from collection point to addressee, below some specified weight and/or minimum threshold price of carriage.

*Natural Monopoly:* A situation where there are either ECONOMIES OF SCALE or SCOPE, or both, but these are only relevant where they prevail at output levels which are large relative to market demand. (*See* Waterson, 1988, Ch. 2, for a much tighter definition.)

*Overhead Costs:* Costs of production which cannot be allocated to a particular service, i.e. those costs which are not AVOIDABLE COSTS.

*Parcel:* Legal definitions vary, but usually a postal item above some specified weight (often 500 grammes) which may or may not be TIME SENSITIVE.

*Post Town:* A geographical area, based on a town, in which mail service is regarded as 'local delivery'.

*Predatory Pricing:* Where a service-provider holds the price of an item below its AVOIDABLE COST in an attempt to force competitors out of the market.

*Premium Mail:* Mail which requires special handling regarding one or more of speed of delivery, guaranteed delivery, personal delivery or physical care. (*See* also COURIER, EXPRESS MAIL and TIME-SENSITIVE MAIL.)

*Primary Distribution:* A term used by Rowland Hill to describe mail carried within or between POST TOWNS. (*See* also SECONDARY DISTRIBUTION.)

*Ramsey-Boiteux Pricing:* Where the different services are priced so as to cover all costs (AVOIDABLE and OVERHEAD) with the least cost to economic efficiency. This involves having relatively large mark-ups on marginal costs for those services with relatively inelastic demands. This idea was originally developed by the British economist, Ramsey, in relation to efficient commodity taxation, and was applied to public utility pricing by the French economist, Boiteux.

**Remail:** Where mail is carried privately from country A for posting in the official system of country B for distribution in country A (ABA), country B (ABB) or country C (ABC). This will occur when it is cheaper to remail than post in A's official system, perhaps because of bulk discounts offered by B's postal administration. (*See* Gröner and Knorr, 1990, for elaboration.)

**Secondary Distribution:** A term used by Rowland Hill for mail originating from and/or addressed to areas which are not part of a POST TOWN. (*See* also PRIMARY DISTRIBUTION.)

**Single Market:** A situation where any buyer in a geographical area (e.g. the EC) can buy from any seller in the area without restriction (or any seller can sell to any buyer). (Note: This is not the meaning of the term adopted by the authors of the *Green Paper*.)

**Sunk Costs:** Those costs which, once incurred, cannot be retrieved. The absence of significant sunk costs is important for CONTESTABILITY of a NATURAL MONOPOLY.

**Terminal Dues:** The charges made by an official postal service for handling the mail emanating from another country's official postal service. These have tended to have been set below AVOIDABLE COSTS and have been based on the aggregate weight of items carried rather than the number and weight of individual items. They have been administered by the UNIVERSAL POSTAL UNION.

**Time-Sensitive Mail:** Very similar to EXPRESS MAIL or PREMIUM MAIL.

**Uniform Price:** A pricing system where the price of a mail item within a geographical area is the same irrespective of from where it emanates or to where it is sent within that area.

**Universal Postal Union:** The international body, based in Berne, Switzerland, which was formed in 1874 to develop common rules for the exchange of mail between the official postal services of the member countries. It has approximately 170 members. It is responsible for administering the system of TERMINAL DUES. (*See* Campbell, 1991, for elaboration.)

# References

Adam Smith Institute (1991): *The Last Post*, ASI Watching Brief, London: ASI.

Albon, R. P. (1987): *Privatise the Post: Steps Towards a Competitive Postal Service*, Policy Study No. 82, London: Centre for Policy Studies.

Albon, R. P. (1990): 'Aspects of Postal Pricing Efficiency in Japan', Report to Institute for Posts and Telecommunications Policy, Tokyo, November.

Albon, R. P. (1991a): 'Postal Rate-Making Procedures and Outcomes in Various Countries', in Crew and Kleindorfer, *op. cit.*, pp. 233-49.

Albon, R. P. (1991b): *Postal Monopoly in Europe: The End in Sight?*, London: Aims of Industry.

Beesley, M. E., and B. Laidlaw (1989): *The Future of Telecommunications*, Research Monograph 42, London: Institute of Economic Affairs.

Berg, S. V., and J. Tschirhart (1988): *Natural Monopoly Regulation: Principles and Practice*, Cambridge: Cambridge University Press.

Bishop, M. R., and J. A. Kay (1988): *Does Privatization Work? Lessons from the UK*, Centre for Business Strategy, London: London Business School.

Brown, S. J., and D. S. Sibley (1986): *The Theory of Public Utility Pricing*, Cambridge: Cambridge University Press.

Campbell, J. I. (1991): 'International Postal Reform: An Application of the Principles of Rowland Hill to the International Postal System', in Crew and Kleindorfer, *op. cit.*, pp. 17-31.

Clarke, P. (1988): 'Opening up the Post Office', London: Aims of Industry.

Coase, R. H. (1939): 'Rowland Hill and the Penny Post', *Economica*, Vol. 6, November, pp. 423-35.

Commission of the European Parliament (1990): 'Working Paper— Policy Proposals', Document for Senior Officials Group on Posts, Doc 90/035, Brussels.

Corby, M. (1990): 'The Post Office: A Discussion Paper', London: Centre for Policy Studies.

Crew, M. A., and P. R. Kleindorfer (eds.) (1991): *Competition and Innovation in Postal Services*, Boston, Mass.: Kluwer Academic Publishers.

Daunton, M. J. (1985): *Royal Mail: The Post Office Since 1840*, London: Athlone Press.

Department of Trade and Industry (1990): *Competition and Choice: Telecommunications Policy for the 1990s*, A Consultative Document, Cm. 1303, London: HMSO, November.

Dobbs, I., and P. Richards (1991): 'Assessing the Welfare Effects of Entry into Letter Delivery', in Crew and Kleindorfer, *op. cit.*, pp. 61-87.

Estrin, S., and D. de Meza (1990): 'The Postal Monopoly: A Case Study', *Economic Review*, Vol. 7, No. 3, January, pp. 2-7.

Estrin, S., and D. de Meza (1991): 'Delivering Letters: Should it be Decriminalized?', in Crew and Kleindorfer, *op. cit.*, pp. 93-108.

Gröner, H., and A. Knorr (1990): 'Cooperation and Competition in National Postal Services' (in German), International Conference on the Future of Postal Services in Europe, Bonn, October.

Haldi, J. (1974): *Postal Monopoly: An Assessment of the Private Express Statutes*, Evaluative Studies 13, Washington DC: American Enterprise Institute.

Harvey, G. (1990): 'A Postal Strategy in a Global Market', International Conference on the Future of Postal Services in Europe, Bonn, October.

Higgs, H. (ed.) (1926): *Palgrave's Dictionary of Political Economy*, London: Macmillan. ('The Post Office', Vol. 3, pp. 173-76.)

Jones, A. (1991): 'Letters in a Bottleneck?', *Direct Marketing International*.

Marshall, A. (1891): Letters to *The Times*, 24 March and 6 April.

Nelson, N. (1990): 'Parcelforce and Product Differentiation', International Conference on the Future of Postal Services in Europe, Bonn, October.

Panzar, J. C. (1991): 'Is Postal Service a Natural Monopoly?', in Crew and Kleindorfer, *op. cit.*, pp. 219-28.

Post Office (1979): *The Letter Monopoly: A Review*, London, October.

Prebble, R. (1989): 'How to Privatise Postal Services: Lessons from New Zealand', Canada Post Privatisation Conference, Toronto, 23 June.

Pryke, R. (1981): *The Nationalised Industries: Policies and Performance since 1968*, Oxford: Martin Robertson. ('Postal Services', Ch. 9.)

Senior, I. (1970): *The Postal Services: Competition or Monopoly?*, Background Memorandum 3, London: Institute of Economic Affairs.

Senior, I. (1983): *Liberating the Letter: A Proposal to Privatise the Post Office*, Research Monograph 38, London: IEA.

Senior, I. (1989): 'Liberating the Letter', in C. Veljanovski (ed.), *Privatisation and Competition: A Market Prospectus*, Hobart Paperback 28, London: Institute of Economic Affairs, pp. 96-109.

Scheepbouwer, A. J. (1990): 'The Reform of the Dutch PTT—First Experiences of PTT Post After Restruction', International Conference on the Future of Postal Services, Bonn, October.

Sherman, R. (1989): *The Regulation of Monopoly*, Cambridge: Cambridge University Press.

Sherman, R. (1990): 'Competition in Postal Service', in Crew and Kleindorfer, *op. cit.*, pp. 191-214.

Tabor, R. (1987): 'Who Benefits from "One Price for Everywhere"?', *Public Finance And Accountancy*, Vol. 12, pp. 44-49.

Tabor, R. (1991): 'Comments: International Postal Reform', in Crew and Kleindorfer, *op. cit.*, pp. 33-36.

Toime, E. (1991): 'Competitive Strategy for New Zealand Post', in Crew and Kleindorfer, *op. cit.*, pp. 275-82.

Waterson, M. (1988): *Regulation of the Firm and Natural Monopoly*, Oxford: Basil Blackwell.

*Of Related Interest*

Summary of Research Monograph 38
# Liberating the Letter
*A proposal to privatise the Post Office*
### IAN SENIOR

1. The origin of the Post Office's statutory letter monopoly lies in government exploitation to raise revenue from what was once the sole, and hence profitable, means of communication.
2. The letter monopoly and uniform nationwide postal tariffs are nowadays defended—not least by the Post Office itself—on the unfounded assumptions that letters are a 'social service' because mail is 'essential' and servicing rural areas is inherently unprofitable.
3. People choose to live in the country in the light of an array of costs which differ from towns; urban dwellers should not be compelled to subsidise rural postal services, which are less 'essential' than food and no more a 'social service' than the village shop or pub.
4. Though the Post Office comes out well on international comparisons, it has allowed its manpower costs to escalate unnecessarily and the quality of its services has deteriorated.
5. Much empirical evidence, such as private initiatives during the 1971 postal strike and the recent expansion of courier services, suggests there is a large volume of private resources keen to serve the postal market if permitted.
6. The Post Office's letter monopoly and its obligation to serve unprofitable rural areas should be removed; the time is now also ripe to separate its mail and counter services and sell both to the public—perhaps offering the staff shares at a discount—as two distinct private companies.
7. The Post Office is currently profitable and has the potential to remain so even without the letter monopoly; the public could be expected to take up the offer of shares in it.
8. With suppliers free to operate commercially and establish market pricing structures, there would be little prospect of postal services disappearing from rural areas. If especially remote communities could not be supplied profitably, local councils could offer subsidies from the rates to attract private operators.
9. The dawning electronic revolution will soon pose a major competitive challenge to both the mail and counter services of the state-owned Post Office whether its paper letter monopoly is removed or not.
10. If the Post Office is to survive the competition from the new technologies and preserve the jobs of postmen and counter clerks, it will require the flexibility and management incentives of the private company.

ISBN 0-255 36164-5 £2.00

**IEA**
**THE INSTITUTE OF ECONOMIC AFFAIRS**
**2 Lord North Street, Westminster**
**London SW1P 3LB    Telephone: 071-799 3745**